HURRICANES

BILL McAULIFFE

WEATHER X BOOKS

CREATIVE EDUCATION · CREATIVE PAPERBACKS

HUR

Published by Creative Education and Creative Paperbacks • P.O. Box 227, Mankato, Minnesota 56002 • Creative Education and Creative Paperbacks are imprints of The Creative Company • www.thecreativecompany.us • Design by Rita Marshall • Production by Christine Vanderbeek • Printed in China • Photographs by Alamy (Chronicle, FEMA, Eric Gevaert, Mike Hill, J Marshall – Tribaleye Images, Karen & Ian Stewart, National Geographic Creative, Peter Charlesworth, RGB Ventures/SuperStock, Oleg Shpak), Corbis (Smiley N. Pool), Getty Images (Buyenlarge, larryrains), iStockphoto (Craig McCausland), Shutterstock (helloseeds, Mike Theiss), SuperStock (Photoshot Holdings Ltd, Reuters, Photobank gallery), Zacarias Pereira da Mata (NASA)

Library of Congress Cataloging-in-Publication Data • Names: McAuliffe, Bill, author. • Title: Hurricanes / Bill McAuliffe. • Series: X-Books: Weather. • Includes bibliographical references and index.
Summary: A countdown of five of the most devastating hurricanes provides thrills as readers discover more about the features of this massive, ocean-borne weather phenomenon. • IDENTIFIERS: LCCN 2016059688 / ISBN 978-1-60818-825-3 (HARDCOVER) / ISBN 978-1-62832-428-0 (PBK) / ISBN 978-1-56660-873-2 (EBOOK)
Subjects: LCSH: Hurricanes—Juvenile literature. • CLASSIFICATION: LCC QC944.2.M38 2017 / DDC 551.55/2–dc23
CCSS: RI.3.1–8; RI.4.1–5, 7; RI.5.1–3, 8; RI.6.1–2, 4, 7; RH.6-8.3–8
First Edition HC 9 8 7 6 5 4 3 2 1 • First Edition PBK 9 8 7 6 5 4 3 2 1

R!CANES

CONTENTS

NAMES FOR HURRICANES
AROUND THE WORLD

HURRICANES Atlantic Ocean and northeastern Pacific Ocean

TYPHOONS Indian Ocean and western Pacific Ocean

TROPICAL CYCLONES Indian Ocean and south of the equator

STORM SURGE

XTRAORDINARY WEATHER

Hurricanes are huge storms. Their rains are heavy. Their winds are strong. They can rip up trees and knock down buildings. They can destroy cities and coastlines. Hurricanes are the mightiest storms on Earth.

Hurricane Basics

Hurricanes are members of a family of storms known as tropical cyclones. These storms form over water. They start along the **equator**. In the Northern Hemisphere, they travel northward. In the Southern Hemisphere, they move south.

Hurricanes can travel thousands of miles. Sometimes they wander for weeks. They can take surprising turns. When hurricanes hit land, they bring a wall of water known as a storm surge. This water can rush 30 miles (48.3 km) inland. It often floods cities and farms.

CYCLONES AROUND THE WORLD

EQUATOR

WHEN HURRICANES HIT LAND,

they can cause tornadoes to form.

In 2004, Hurricane Ivan produced

a record 117 tornadoes.

CYCLONES RARELY FORM

in the southern Atlantic.

HURRICANES RARELY FORM

within 300 miles (483 km) of the equator.

All tropical cyclones rotate. Storms north of the equator rotate counterclockwise. South of the equator, they rotate clockwise.

TYPHOON TIP (1979) IS THE LARGEST

tropical cyclone on record.

It was 1,367 miles (2,200 km) wide.

TROPICAL CYCLONE TRACY (1974) IS THE SMALLEST

on record. It was 62.1 miles (100 km) wide.

THE EYE IS CALM

The center of a hurricane is known as the eye.

It can be 20 to 40 miles (32.3–64.4 km) wide.

The storm spins around the eye.

Flooding is usually the most damaging result of a hurricane. The floodwaters carry trash, sewage, and dead animals. That ruins drinking water. It also creates a high risk of injury and disease.

Hurricanes drive people and wildlife from their homes. But they do some good, too. They can bring much-needed rain to dry areas. And they carry heat away from the equator. That spreads tropical warmth to cooler parts of the world.

"Cyclone" means circle or wheel in Greek.

HURRICANES SPIN

HURRICANE BASICS FACT

The average hurricane is 340 miles (547 km) wide

and 9 miles (14.5 km) high.

TOP FIVE XTREME HURRICANES

Xtreme Hurricane #5

The Galveston Hurricane Galveston, Texas, was a thriving city in the late 1800s. It had 40,000 residents. People came to visit its beaches. Many businesses were there, too. But in 1900, a hurricane hit the city. It killed between 8,000 and 12,000 people. It is the deadliest storm in United States history. Its storm surge was more than 15 feet (4.6 m) high. Only a few buildings were left standing. The city had to be rebuilt.

There are many ways to compare hurricanes.

Intensity, size, deaths, cost of damages—

any one of these can earn hurricanes a place in history.

Hurricane Formation

Almost all hurricanes that strike the U.S. begin far to the east. They form over the Atlantic Ocean. These storms get started by dry winds blowing west from Africa. Surface water that is at least 80 °F (27 °C) **evaporates**. The water vapor is carried upward with rising warm air. As it rises, it cools and forms clouds. This often leads to a thunderstorm.

Sometimes a group of thunderstorms forms. This is called a tropical disturbance. These systems continue to rise. They pull up warm air from below. Other air rushes in to replace it. That air rotates. As the storm moves over warm waters, it gets stronger.

Strong, cold winds can cut off the storm's growth. So can stretches of cool ocean water. But some of these storms swell into powerful hurricanes. On land, hurricanes are doomed. Their supply of warm sea air is cut off. The land slows their winds.

TROPICAL DISTURBANCE 125–375 miles (201–604 km) wide

TROPICAL DEPRESSION rotating winds up to 38 miles (61.2 km) per hour

TROPICAL STORM rotating winds between 39 and 73 miles (62.8–117 km) per hour; this is when storms are given a name

HURRICANE 300–400 miles (483–644 km) wide; winds greater than 74 miles (119 km) per hour

The eye wall surrounds the eye. The eye wall has the strongest winds.

It also produces the heaviest rains.

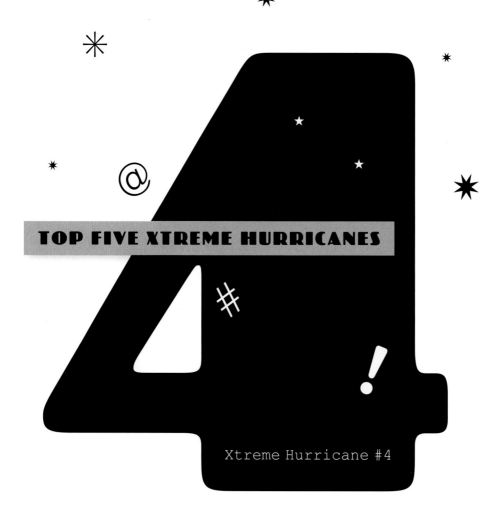

TOP FIVE XTREME HURRICANES

Xtreme Hurricane #4

Hurricane Mitch hit Central America in 1998. It dropped 50 to 75 inches (127–191 cm) of rain on parts of Honduras and Nicaragua. Entire villages were swept away in water and mudslides. More than 11,000 people died. It sank ships, too. Mitch wandered around the Gulf of Mexico. It passed over Florida as a tropical storm. Eventually, the storm died in the Atlantic Ocean.

OCTOBER 26–NOVEMBER 4, 1998

XCEPTIONAL HURRICANES

People love living in warm places along the sea. But so do tropical storms. Hurricanes often hit coastal cities. There, they cause massive damage.

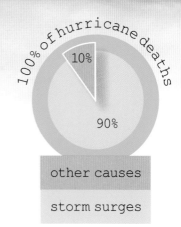

100% of hurricane deaths

10%

90%

other causes

storm surges

HURRICANE OCCURRENCES FACT

The eastern Pacific Ocean, off the coast of North America, has about nine hurricanes each year.

Hurricanes move 15–20 miles (24.1–32.2 km) per hour.

ATLANTIC HURRICANES

Hurricane Occurrences

New Orleans. Bangladesh. The Caribbean islands. Japan. Nicaragua. These places are far from one another. But they are all close to warm seas. And they all share a history of visits from violent tropical cyclones.

Tropical storms form year round in some parts of the world. The northwestern Pacific sees the most in the world. About 26 tropical storms form there each year. Nearly 17 become typhoons. Many of them slam into Japan, China, and Southeast Asia.

The North Atlantic is a distant second. It averages 12 tropical storms a year. Only about six turn into hurricanes. They develop in late summer. That is when conditions are just right. Ocean waters are warm, and winds are light.

XASPERATING STORMS

For centuries, tropical storms have wiped out everything in their paths. They have destroyed armies, cities, forests, and wildlife. Over time, some places are restored. But some remain in ruins.

XASPERATING STORMS FACT

The names of especially disastrous storms are retired. Through 2016, 82 Atlantic hurricane names had been retired.

The National Hurricane Center began using female names for hurricanes in 1953. Male names were added in 1979.

In the 13th century, the ruler Kublai Khan tried twice to invade Japan by sea. But typhoons struck his ships. Hundreds of soldiers drowned. In **colonial** times, the navies of France, Holland, Great Britain, and Spain were battered by Caribbean hurricanes. In 2005, more than one million people fled the Gulf Coast area hit by Hurricane Katrina. Many never returned.

Hurricanes can be hard on plants and animals, too. In 1992, leaves that Hurricane Andrew stripped off trees rotted in the Gulf of Mexico and other bodies of water. That used up the water's oxygen. Fish could not breathe. About 9.4 million fish died in coastal waters. In Louisiana's Atchafalaya Basin, nearly 182 million fish died. But by 1995, some fish populations were almost back to normal.

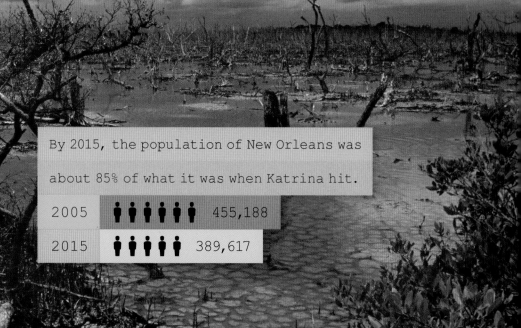

By 2015, the population of New Orleans was about 85% of what it was when Katrina hit.

| 2005 | 👤👤👤👤👤👤 | 455,188 |
| 2015 | 👤👤👤👤👤 | 389,617 |

3

TOP FIVE XTREME HURRICANES

Xtreme Hurricane #3

Hurricane Katrina was the costliest storm in U.S. history. It ran up more than $100 billion in damages. Katrina was a Category 3 storm when it reached the U.S. in 2005. When it hit New Orleans, it was a Category 2. But its 28-foot (8.5 m) storm surge broke dams. The city (already situated below sea level) quickly flooded. In some places, water stood 12 feet (3.7 m) deep. About 2,000 people died.

AUGUST 29, 2005

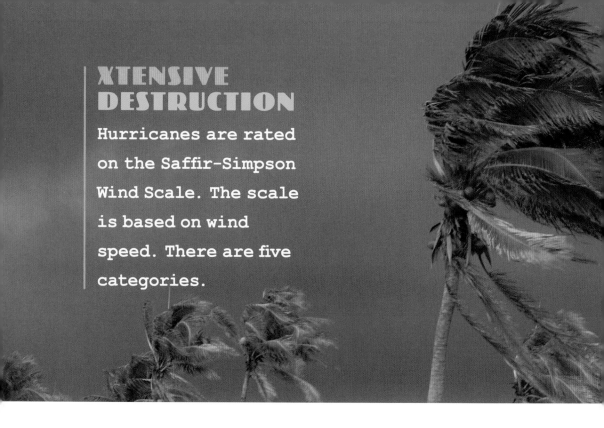

XTENSIVE DESTRUCTION

Hurricanes are rated on the Saffir-Simpson Wind Scale. The scale is based on wind speed. There are five categories.

Hurricane Categories

Category 1 and 2 storms have the weakest winds. Hurricanes are considered major when they reach Category 3. A Category 5 storm is the worst. Damages associated with each category are also ranked. They range from minimal (Category 1) to catastrophic (Categories 4 and 5).

All hurricanes can cause extensive damage. Most knock out power. Winds can snap trees in half. Storm surges rush over land. It can take days for floodwaters to withdraw. Buildings are damaged. Homes are destroyed. Mass evacuation is often recommended, or even required. When these extreme storms hit, destruction is almost always unavoidable.

Category 1	74–95 miles (119–153 km) per hour
Category 2	96–110 miles (154–177 km) per hour
Category 3	111–129 miles (178–208 km) per hour
Category 4	130–156 miles (209–251 km) per hour
Category 5	greater than 156 miles (251 km) per hour

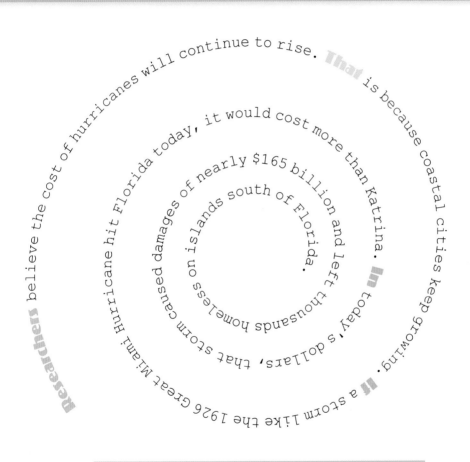

Researchers believe the cost of hurricanes will continue to rise. That is because coastal cities keep growing. If a storm like the 1926 Great Miami Hurricane hit Florida today, it would cost more than Katrina. In today's dollars, that storm caused damages of nearly $165 billion and left thousands homeless on islands south of Florida.

HURRICANE CATEGORIES FACT

The Great Miami Hurricane was a Category 4 storm. Few residents were prepared for the storm. Much of the city was destroyed.

Xtreme Hurricane #2

The Great Hurricane of 1780 devastated the Caribbean. It hit Barbados first. About 4,300 people died there. Nearly every building was leveled. On St. Lucia, about 6,000 people were killed. Another 9,000 died on Martinique. Between 4,000 and 5,000 died on St. Eustatius. Ships sank at sea. Many people drowned. Then the storm moved north to Florida. It remains the deadliest storm the Western Hemisphere has ever seen.

OCTOBER 10–16, 1780

A hurricane is categorized by its strongest wind gust. The wind must last for at least one minute.

Some hurricanes have enough power to meet 20 percent of the world's energy needs for a year.

The most active Atlantic hurricane season was 2005. Of the 15 hurricanes that formed, 7 were Category 3 or higher.

The eye of a hurricane is often sunny.

Causing $75 billion in damages, Hurricane Sandy (2012) was the second-costliest hurricane in U.S. history.

In 2002, Hurricane Andrew was upgraded from Category 4 to Category 5 before it struck land.

Some hurricanes start off the western coast of Mexico and move out to the Pacific.

Three hurricanes have hit the U.S. as Category 5 storms: the "Labor Day" hurricane (1935), Hurricane Camille (1969), and Hurricane Andrew (1992).

Hurricane Wilma (2005) had the smallest eye of any Atlantic hurricane in history.

In 1994, Hurricane John traveled 8,188 miles (13,177 km) in 30 days. Its distance and time set records.

The warmest air in a hurricane is near the top of the eye.

Scientists fly planes into the paths of hurricanes to study them.

In 2015, Hurricane Patricia's winds topped 200 miles (322 km) per hour.

Some tropical storm

ravel over Central America, from the Atlantic to the Pacific.

NOVEMBER 12, 1970

Xtreme Hurricane #1

The Great Bhola Cyclone crashed into Bangladesh in 1970. Its storm surge was 20 to 30 feet (6.1–9.1 m) high. At least 300,000 people died. It was the deadliest storm in recorded history. The country has a lot of low-lying land. The shape of the coastline funnels cyclones toward it. In the 20th century, seven of the nine deadliest storms in the world hit Bangladesh. All were cyclones.

GLOSSARY

colonial – describing the period when European countries controlled areas in North America, from the 1500s to the 1700s

equator – the imaginary line around the center of the globe, halfway between the North and South poles

evaporates – changes from a liquid to a gas

typhoon – a tropical storm that forms in the Indian or western Pacific oceans

RESOURCES

Emanuel, Kerry. *Divine Wind: The History and Science of Hurricanes*. New York: Oxford University Press, 2005.

Lynch, John. *The Weather*. Buffalo, N.Y.: Firefly Books, 2002.

National Oceanic and Atmospheric Administration: National Hurricane Center. "Hurricanes in History." http://www.nhc.noaa .gov/outreach/history/.

Norcross, Bryan. *Hurricane Almanac: The Essential Guide to Storms Past, Present, and Future*. New York: St. Martin's Griffin, 2007.

INDEX

Hurricanes do not form on the equator or cross over it.